LOGIC TO BELIEF

Elizabeth Napier

Saved in Christ Publications

Logic to Belief

Copyright © 2023 by Elizabeth Napier

All rights reserved.
No portion of this book may be reproduced in any form without written permission from the publisher or author except as permitted by U.S. Copyright law. This publication is designed to provide opinions and information in regard to the subject matter covered. All opinions expressed herein are the sole opinion of the author. It is sold with the understanding that neither the author nor the publisher is engaged in rendering legal, investment, accounting, mental health or other professional services. While the publisher and author have used their best efforts in preparing this book, they make no representations or warranties with respect to the accuracy or completeness of the contents of this book and specifically disclaim any implied warranties of merchantability or fitness for a particular purpose. No warranty may be created or extended by sales representatives or written sales materials. The advice and strategies contained herein may not be suitable for your situation. You should consult with a professional when appropriate. Neither the publisher nor the author shall be liable for any loss of profit or any other commercial damage, or any other damages, including but not limited to special, incidental, consequential, personal, or other damages.

Published in Carleton, MI by Saved in Christ Publications. For fundraising opportunities, wholesale purchase, or educational use please email savedsisterinchrist@gmail.com.

ISBN: 979-8-9881040-0-1
Library of Congress Control Number: 2023905795

Cover and interior design: Elizabeth Napier. Cover Image by Enrique from Pixabay.

1 2 3 4 5 6 7 8 9 10

This book is dedicated to my husband, William, and children, Molly, Graham, and Gwendolyn, for putting up with me while I write and listen to praise music all day long

to my father and mother for teaching me so much about life and love

and most importantly, to God for sending His Son to save me and filling me with His Holy Spirit so that I might be inspired by Him to help others.

Table of Contents

Introduction..7
The Exercise...19
But What About?...33
So What Now?..44
The Principles..47
Principle 1..49
Principle 2..54
Principle 3..60
Principle 4..68
Principle 5..74
Principle 6..81
Principle 7..88
Principle 8..94
Principle 9..100
I Finished! What Next?...............................109

1
INTRODUCTION

"We take 100,000,000 silver dollars and lay them on the face of Texas. They will cover all of the state two feet deep. Now mark one of these silver dollars and stir the whole mass thoroughly...Blindfold a man and tell him...he must pick up one silver dollar...What chance would he have of getting the right one? Just the same chance that the prophets would have of writing...eight prophecies and having them come true in any one man."
- Josh McDowell, *More Than a Carpenter*

"Scientific accuracy confirms the Bible is the Word of God."
- Adrian Rodgers

I like to think of myself as a relatively logical person. Not being a great athlete, or a talented artist, I have instead always prided myself on doing well in school. I was skilled at things like reading, getting good grades, qualifying for gifted programs, and taking tests. I have earned degrees from the University of Michigan (a Bachelor of Arts in Psychology), the University of San Diego School of Law (a Juris Doctorate with a full ride scholarship!), and Sierra Nevada University (a Master of Arts in Teaching). I enjoy doing logic puzzles in my spare time; I have ever since I was a kid. I love reading and learning, and I try to be open to understanding new things. I'll admit I can be a pretty annoying person with all of my random trivial facts, but I'm working on doing better!

So, when I approached a point in my life where I decided I had to figure out what exactly it is that I believe about an afterlife and God, I knew that I wasn't going to be convinced by the arguments of one side or another. When people argued about the Bible in the comments sections of the internet, I knew one of them must be correct and one of them must be incorrect, but I honestly had no idea which was which. In order to satisfy my own curiosity, I would have to just go right to the source material - the Bible. I would finally have to read it for myself, instead of just quickly searching for random Bible verses that mentioned something that seemed like it might help my argument. Sometimes I would be arguing that the Bible was bad, sometimes good, but the truth was, I really had no idea what I was talking about. I had no firm set of beliefs and no foundation for whatever beliefs I did have.

It was shameful to realize that for as many books as I had read, at 46 years old, I had never just sat down and read the Bible. Yet I had no problem judging others based on what I assumed it said, or acting like I knew more about what it said than I did. I also had no problem learning about other things. I loved reading, learning about other religions, holidays, inventions, important people throughout history, and so on...so it made no sense at all that I never bothered to read the Bible. It was finally time to do something about it.

And I did it! I followed through and read every word, more than once. When I initially decided to read the Bible, I don't really know what I was expecting. I guess I thought one way or another, I would discover for myself what was real and true. I grew up as a child going to church with my family. I knew all of the routines and prayers, and I thought I knew most of the Bible stories. I quit going to church as I got older and didn't really pursue much in the way of religion, other than praying when I was scared, until I was about 44-45 years old. My teenage daughter started to take an interest in attending church, which eventually prompted my curiosity to read the Bible. And something began happening as I finally commenced reading it for myself. My eyes were opened to so much more than just the words on the page, and I realized its truth.

I will discuss my personal experiences in a little more detail throughout this book, but I don't want that to become the main focus. My sincere hope is that what you read on these next few pages will inspire you to pick up a copy of the Bible and find out for yourself what it says and what it means. So that is why we are going to quickly get right into the main inspiration for writing this. God is putting forth the premise that there is no logical reason to deny His existence. There is no downside to believing in God, and there is no downside to reading the Bible, if you consider the final outcome.

There are plenty of logical arguments to make when debating the veracity of the Bible. For example, many people like to argue that science disproves the creationism claims. Let's just quickly take a look at two of the most well-known origin-related theories at a base level. We will not spend more than a brief moment on the counter arguments to these theories, for although they may be important and helpful, they are not the main focus of this book. In addition, it is important to note that anything labeled by science as a theory has never actually been proven to be true. In my husband's opinion, the sheer absurdity of the things we must believe in order to assume the truth of the following two theories alone is enough to prove the claims of the Bible.

The Big Bang Theory: This theory is that two lifeless rocks formed out of nothing in a giant explosion, crashed into one another, and then a chunk of one of them eventually moved into an exactly perfect distance and orbit from the sun. The moon somehow also formed and became a perfect orbit and distance from the Earth to support life. Water and the sun somehow also appeared on their own from all of that nothing. And then somehow, over time, nearly two million different varieties of plant and animal life forms grew from one cell on that lifeless rock. And to our current scientific knowledge this has never happened on any other planet that we can find. To me, this theory seems way more far-fetched than believing in creation by God. Looking at the precision of it all, the theory that makes more sense is that life was planned and all matter was formed by an intelligent creator. But anyone who believes in the Big Bang Theory has no right to call Biblical claims outlandish. Especially when you look at the next theory combined with it.

The Theory of Evolution: So if we believe life started from one cell, then we also have to believe this theory. Somehow the 900,000 different kinds of insects that currently exist on this planet evolved from that cell, along with about 5400 different mammal varieties, 11,900 reptile types, 10,000 bird species and over 30,000 kinds of fish. Oh yeah, don't forget the 250,000 plus varieties of plants.[1] That is a LOT of evolution from one cell; it seems like we would be seeing evidence of evolution everywhere. But we still can't prove this theory. How did one cell become both animal and plant, and so many different kinds of each? Seems like one creator makes much more sense. That, or we share a common ancestor with celery.

To my knowledge, NONE of the theories about the origin of the universe have been proven by science. In fact, I'm pretty certain that, throughout history, "science" has been wrong about things more often than it has been right, which makes us kind of silly to put all our trust in it. Our textbooks constantly need to be updated to add new information or to remove outdated former facts. Things we were once taught (e.g. margarine is healthier than butter, eat low-fat, Pluto is a planet) change over time as we continue to unravel the mysteries of life. Medicines promoted by science turn out to kill or disfigure (Thalidomide anyone?), machines designed by engineers fail and have defects, weather predictions made by

---

[1] Species numbers found at www.nwf.org and www.si.edu through a Google search.

meteorologists are still repeatedly incorrect. Unless it is something common, doctors can take years to figure out how to help, and often misdiagnose people. Not to mention the influx of private interest money poured into scientific "research" which often leads to some questionable results. We want to act as if people who believe in God and the Bible are somehow lacking intelligence or discernment, but I do not see how the biblical creation explanation comes across as sounding any more implausible than the scientific theories.

    Another logical argument is that we can test the veracity of the Bible by checking to see if any of the prophetic statements made within its pages ever came true. The initial quote at the start of this chapter is referencing the odds of one person fulfilling just eight of the biblical prophecies regarding Jesus Christ. It is basically impossible. When you consider that there were actually hundreds of biblical prophecies that predict the person of Jesus Christ, including ones that precisely describe his birth and death, it is mind-blowing. If anyone today could make predictions with such startling accuracy, people would pay fortunes to have them tell their future. This fact alone is more proof of the truth of Biblical claims than exists for any of the scientific theories.

Anyway, while those are all interesting discussions to have, they are not the topic of this book. I am sure there are other people out there who have written, or preached, or vlogged about these topics before. I do not claim any special credit for the following ideas because God just gave me the realization that there is no logical reason to not believe in Him, and it is now my duty to explain what this means. If other people have also been sharing that message, please continue to spread the word. People will listen to and understand a message from one person, but then be completely confused by a similar message from someone else. We all have different writing and communication styles and readers may prefer one over another. The more voices the better!

When I first started writing, I thought I was going to publish this online as a blog. I didn't think I would really have enough inspiration to write an entire book. But this is where God comes into the picture. When He inspires and directs, I have learned it is our job to follow and so here I am, turning this blog into a book. Because of this, my style of writing may tend to reflect the informal nature of a blog post rather than a book. I hope you will not find it too distracting.

I also want this book to become something that helps to guide you toward the first steps in learning and understanding what God's message is to the world. This book can really be separated into two sections: a) the logic exercise and b) principles to learning more. I hope you will find the principles that follow the logic exercise helpful as you work through your own thoughts related to these issues. Feel free to write notes directly in the book as you are reading, I have included space for notes, but please write in the margins, highlight, do as you please; it is your book.

Lastly, as with any book dealing with a controversial topic, I am sure there will be many critics worrying about specific words I used, or twisting these ideas and taking things out of context. It is not my job to worry about any of that. My only purpose is to get you started on the path to thinking about eternity. It is my opinion that you cannot make a decision without making an effort to educate yourself. While it would be amazing if this book convinced someone to give their lives to God, the main goal is just to get as many people as possible to think for themselves, instead of letting the world think for them. To encourage people to think logically through these arguments, read the evidence, and make their own choice. If that offends someone, I would have to question why they would think that knowledge, critical thinking, and logic-based decision making are such bad things.

All of that being said, let's go ahead and jump right into the logic exercise. If you have ever taken a logic, philosophy, or law course, you may be relatively familiar with this type of exercise. However, even if you have not, it should be simple enough to follow.

Notes

2
THE EXERCISE

"I am trying here to prevent anyone saying the really foolish thing that people often say about Him: I'm ready to accept Jesus as a great moral teacher, but I don't accept his claim to be God. That is the one thing we must not say. A man who was merely a man and said the sort of things Jesus said would not be a great moral teacher. He would either be a lunatic — on the level with the man who says he is a poached egg — or else he would be the Devil of Hell. You must make your choice. Either this man was, and is, the Son of God, or else a madman or something worse. You can shut him up for a fool, you can spit at him and kill him as a demon or you can fall at his feet and call him Lord and God, but let us not come with any patronizing nonsense about his being a great human teacher. He has not left that open to us. He did not intend to."
- C.S. Lewis

PROBLEM 1

Directions:

- Read and imagine what happens to the people in each of these two scenarios.
- Follow them through to their logical outcomes.
- Determine which outcomes are preferable (rank outcomes or determine positive and negative ratings).
- Form a conclusion based on which choice is logically most likely to lead to the best possible outcome.

My assertion is that as you work through this exercise, you will discover why it makes complete logical sense to believe in what the Bible says about God and eternal life. I claim it is by far the less risky choice. There is no downside!

Scenario:

Suppose there are two people, Person A and Person B, who are both about to die. Your job is to determine whose belief system has the greatest chance of producing the most desired outcome. Disclaimer: None of the people in the following scenarios are intended to represent any actual or fictional person or religion and are merely examples of general beliefs that people may hold.

Person A: Person A believes 100 percent in God, and that we all have eternal life. Person A believes that we have a choice to follow God and spend our eternal life rewarded as his adopted children, or to choose not to follow Him, and then suffer our eternal life in torture, separated from God.

Person B: Does not believe in any afterlife. B believes that whatever we do in this life is all that there is, and that once it is over, there is nothing else. We all equally just rot into the ground with no more consciousness. The only rewards you will receive are what you are able to obtain here and now.

Questions to think about:

Stop and make note of your answers to the following questions, and record your thoughts and feelings as you evaluate this scenario. Refer back to the directions to guide you through the steps to take in your thought processes.

- What happens to these two people who are going to die soon?
- What happens to each of them when they die if Person A is Correct?
- What happens to each of them when they die if Person B is correct?
- Imagine each of those things happening to you when you die. How do you and your family and friends personally feel about each outcome and which is preferable?

Notes

SOLUTION
✷✷Spoiler alert✷✷

My solution to the above scenario follows on the next page. If you would like to take some time to work through this scenario on your own, do not turn the page yet! Remember to refer back to the directions and questions from the previous scenario to guide your thinking.

"Atheism is so senseless. When I look at the solar system, I see the earth at the right distance from the sun to receive the proper amounts of heat and light. This did not happen by chance."
- Sir Isaac Newton

Outcomes:

If Person A is correct, and God is real, these are the possible outcomes:
- Person A will have a rewarded eternal life with God, and will convince Person B to join them so they can both live rewarded for eternity.
- Person A will have a rewarded life with God, but Person B will spend an eternal life in torment and separated from God.

If Person B is correct, and there is no afterlife, then this is the only possible outcome:
- Both Person B and Person A suffer the same fate, which is they just die, with no consciousness from that point on.

Ranking/rating outcomes:

Only one of these outcomes is ok with me.
1. Eternal life rewarded with God - positive
2. Nothing no consciousness - negative/neutral
3. Eternal life in torture separated from God - negative

Discussion:

First of all, we should be able to agree that the ratings we assign to each of the possible outcomes is entirely subjective. Every individual reading this book will have a slightly different opinion as to where each outcome falls on the sliding scale of positivity or negativity. I may feel that outcome #2 is 99% negative, while you might feel that it is 75% positive, and someone else may think it is 50/50. Although I did not conduct a full-scale survey, based on the people I interact with and my own personal feelings, I believe the majority would generally agree with my ratings.

That being said, if someone reading has a completely different rating of the outcomes (for example, they believe suddenly ceasing to exist is preferable to eternal peace) then while their chances for a positive outcome increase, their chances for a negative do not decrease. This holds true because I am making the assumption that all of us would agree that eternal damnation would not be a positive by any definition. Thus, even if someone rates nothingness as a positive, they can only achieve that outcome if their belief is correct. If Person A is correct, the person who believes in nothingness will face the negative outcome of eternal damnation. But either way, Person A will obtain a positive outcome according to that rating preference, since both nothingness and eternal peace in Heaven would both be considered positive.

According to *my* ratings, the only way to obtain a possible positive outcome upon death is to choose Person A's beliefs and follow God. Choosing Person B's beliefs can only possibly lead to a negative/neutral or negative outcome. Since Person B goes to death not believing in God, he will either simply disappear/cease to exist (negative/neutral), or he will suffer and spend an eternity in torture (negative). Person A on the other hand, will either obtain rewards for eternity (a clear positive in my book), or like Person B, simply cease to exist (negative/neutral).

In addition, Person B would face no eternal consequences if they chose to read the Bible and believe in God. The only real earthly consequence would be the small opportunity cost of the time spent reading and investigating versus doing something else with that time.

However, the eternal consequences of not considering a belief in God, if true, are extremely terrifying. I wouldn't want anyone I know to spend an eternity in torment.

But what about the other downsides? The more immediate concerns? How do Person A and B spend their life on earth? Don't people who follow God have to follow a bunch of restrictive rules? Isn't that a huge downside for Person A?

I think you will find that when you take the time to read the Bible and learn what God wants for your life, you might be surprised at what He requires. God does set forth commandments, and He does desire that we all stop sinning, not because He wants to deprive us, but because our sins always hurt other people or ourselves in some way. When we sin, it also makes us more vulnerable to distance from, and disbelief in, God, because we feel unworthy, or like we are too bad to ever be forgiven by God. I can assure you that forgiveness is always possible, and He will work on your life with you, if you let Him.

People like Person A find so much more fulfillment and joy and peace in life because of their walk with God. Person A has no desire to do all of the things they may have done in the past. They are trusting in the promise of God and are content to follow Him and live as He provides. Person A doesn't see sinful behavior as fun anymore, and is willing to work on giving up things that are harmful in order to receive blessings in eternity. They lose their desire to sin because of their relationship with Jesus and His Holy Spirit. These topics are discussed in more detail in the remaining books in this series, should you find yourself seeking more information.

If Person B is right, they will die and become nothing (same as Person A), but while alive they can pretty much do whatever makes them feel best. If there is no afterlife, there is no motive to do anything other than survive and enjoy the here and now. Some people may see that as a perk, hedonism with no consequences! I used to have somewhat of a similar mindset, not wanting to take the time to really learn about what God wants, because I was worried I would have to change my lifestyle too much. I liked going out and drinking excessively with my friends, I always yearned for more money and respect, the perfect marriage and children. Eventually I realized that living life in that way, at least for me, felt like

I was living an unfulfilled stressed out life. I was always worried about something, rushing from one place to the next, keeping up with social pressures, barely sleeping, angry at everything. In those moments, everything I was doing seemed like it was important, or helping me, but in reality it was making it worse. Since I found God, I cannot explain the amazing peace, joy and fulfillment that brings. I feel like I am living a completely new life.

I also don't like the idea of a world where no one believes there might be eternal consequences for their actions, otherwise we are at the mercy of the individual morality of each person around us. Rules and laws only really matter if you get caught by some person who has more authority and power than you. People without a belief in eternal consequences for their actions may assume they have nothing to fear as long as no one catches them. And in the end, Person B, if correct, will only succeed in achieving the same result as Person A and everyone else: dying and becoming nothing. However! If Person B is wrong, and Person A is correct, Person B may live an eternal life in torture.

Which way sounds better?

Conclusion:

I will not be doing any formal calculations of probability here. I'm sure someone else will, or already has! However, based on my preference ratings, it is clear that Person A's beliefs have the highest probability of a positive outcome. Since, in my opinion, that is the only outcome that has a positive result, the only means of obtaining a positive outcome are through following Person A's beliefs. Person B's beliefs can only possibly lead to a neutral or negative outcome. A 50% chance is better than a 0% chance!

Therefore, it makes logical sense to pursue a belief in God vs a belief in no afterlife. There's no risk to believing in God and learning more about how to follow Him. Death means either eternal Heaven, or nothing. But there is a huge downside to atheism, because death means either nothing, or eternal torture, neither of which sound like my first choice.

Notes

3
But what about...?

"Trusting testimony is not an irrational act of faith that leaves critical rationality aside; it is, on the contrary, the rationally appropriate way of responding to authentic testimony. Gospels understood as testimony are the entirely appropriate means of access to the historical reality of Jesus."
- Richard Bauckham

Problem 2

I am sure a few of you are making the argument that there are more than just these two viewpoints or ideas about religion. What happens if we consider other beliefs? Does the same logic apply? Again, my intention is to represent a general common belief system, not a particular person or religion.

Scenario:
Ok, let's imagine a third person, Person C.

Person C: Person C believes that we continually are reincarnated, living life over and over again until we learn to get things right. We are not consciously aware of these reincarnations. Potentially, if the person makes the right choices, they could reach a transformed state of consciousness. They do not maintain their independent selves in this shared consciousness, where they experience reality independent of the material world.

Questions to think about:
- What happens to these two people who are going to die soon?
- What happens to each of them when they die if Person C is correct?
- Imagine each of those things happening to you when you die. How do you and your family and friends personally feel about each outcome and which is preferable?
- Does adding Person C's beliefs to the mix change the possibility of obtaining a positive or negative outcome?

Notes

SOLUTION
✹ ✹ Spoiler alert ✹ ✹

My solution to the above scenario follows on the next page. If you would like to take some time to work through this scenario on your own, do not turn the page yet! Remember to refer back to the directions and questions from the previous scenario to guide your thinking.

"I've experienced His presence in the deepest darkest hell that men can create. I have tested the promises of the Bible, and believe me, you can count on them. I know that Jesus Christ can live in you, in me, through His Holy Spirit. You can talk with Him; you can talk with Him out loud or in your heart when you are alone, as I was alone in solitary confinement. The joy is that He hears each word."
- Corrie Ten Boom

Outcomes:

If Person A is correct, and God is real, these are the possible outcomes:

- Person A will have a rewarded eternal life with God, and will convince Person B to join them so they can both live rewarded for eternity.
- Person A will have a rewarded life with God, but Person C will spend an eternal life in torment separated from God.

If Person C is correct, then these are the possible outcomes:

- Reincarnation - Both Person C and Person A will likely go through several reincarnations. Every time they die, they will begin living life over and over again as different people. They will experience a new earthly life with all of its happiness as well as all of its pain. Neither one of them will know that they have lived other lives in the past. This possible outcome could conceivably go on forever.
- Obtaining a shared state of transformed consciousness - The hope is at some point either Person A or C, or some combination of their essences, may reform into a new consciousness

that reaches the highest state of enlightenment, but their current selves will not likely be aware of it.

Ranking/rating outcomes:

Once again, only one of these outcomes is ok with me.

1. Eternal life rewarded with God - positive
2. Continuous reincarnation - negative/neutral
3. Obtaining a shared state of transformed consciousness - neutral, my preference is negative. This outcome may be positive or negative depending on your comfort level with the various options for defining this state of transformed consciousness, as well as the recognition that your current consciousness may cease to exist to become part of a larger consciousness. In addition, since you might not obtain this heightened consciousness in this particular lifetime, Person C cannot be 100% positive they will obtain this goal, unlike like Person A with outcome #1.
4. Eternal life in torture separated from God - negative

Discussion:

At first, it seems like Person C has an equal opportunity for a positive outcome. However, the idea of losing my current consciousness to be reborn over and over again does not sound appealing when you think about it. Having to go through life over and over again until we get it right, never knowing when you will reach the point where you can obtain *rest*? This one lifetime has already been difficult, I'm not sure I want to keep living new lives, with no clue where I might end up next.

Ok, I understand that we have to learn, but then what happens after we reach the ultimate goal of Person C's beliefs? Well, there are different views on exactly what happens, but the largest consensus seems to be that we all form, or become part of, a master consciousness. Again, this just sounds weird to me and not preferable to outcome #1. I want to know when I have reached my eternal life. I do not relish the idea of losing myself to meld into one consciousness. Furthermore, how are we learning if we cannot remember the mistakes we made in our past lives?

I am sure there may be people who disagree with my ranking/values assigned, and believe that outcome #3 is positive. So let's go with that and agree for the purposes of argument. Assuming it is a positive outcome, what are Person C's chances of obtaining that outcome, instead of outcome #2? Unfortunately, we can never really know. This also assumes that Person C is correct so that outcome #4 is not possible. This still does not work out to a net positive effect for Person C since there is no way of being certain that this incarnation will be the one where they finally obtain outcome #3. They clearly have not gotten there so far, as they are living this current life, which also means they have already lived through several incarnations over hundreds of years. Calculating the odds that this time will be their last incarnation is practically impossible, since each person never knows what they have done in their past lives to know if they have made any progress.

Conclusion:

If these types of exercises are something you find interesting, by all means, continue through with any other possible scenarios you can think of. To my knowledge, I cannot think of any other set of beliefs that logically offer a better chance at a positive outcome upon death.

In my experience, after reading the Bible and discovering my relationship with God, I can know, with certainty, that I will spend eternity with God. It seems to me that nothing else can promise that certainty of a positive outcome. Therefore, at the very least, the logical person knows it makes sense to investigate and learn about Person A's beliefs for yourself. Of course, if you vehemently disagree with my opinions on the value assigned to each possible outcome, then the rest of this book is probably not of much interest to you! If, however, your curiosity has been piqued, please continue!

Notes

4
So What Now?

"I enter a most earnest plea that in our hurried and rather bustling life of today we do not lose the hold that our forefathers had on the Bible. I wish to see the Bible study as much a matter of course in the secular colleges as in the seminary. No educated man can afford to be ignorant of the Bible, and no uneducated man can afford to be ignorant of the Bible."
  - Theodore Roosevelt

Logic shows that the best path forward is to investigate and pursue a belief in God. If by working through these exercises, you also have come to find this to be true, you may be wondering what exactly that means for you personally. I assume that if you are reading this book, you might not have initially had a firm conviction on your beliefs in an afterlife or God. Perhaps these exercises have you considering your beliefs for the first time. I also assume that many of you are like I was, and have never thoroughly read the entire Bible. All I can tell you is that since I took my first steps toward God, my world has not been the same.

This is why people like me, who have been called by God, want to tell everyone, because God wants everyone to choose Him! I do not want anyone, including myself, to suffer the fate of Person B, or Person C. Because of the tremendous impact reading the Bible has had on me and my family, my main goal is to encourage everyone to read it. At the very least, I pray that you will educate yourself on what it says. I don't want to judge you, because I was in the same boat. I just want to encourage you to learn what I have learned.

So if the above argument has at all prompted a desire in you to learn more, my suggestion is to make reading the Bible your first step. Reading it does not mean that you have committed to becoming a believer in anything, it is just simply the only way to truly understand what exactly is expected of a person who wants to follow God. In my view, you cannot logically form an opinion or belief on the teachings of God unless you have read the book that purports to be His word.

There are definitely additional or alternative steps you could take to pursuing and investigating a belief in God. However, reading the Bible is the only way that I knew that I could be certain what I learned from others was accurate. If you want to start by attending a church or watching videos about God, those are all great ideas too, and I will discuss them more a little later in this book. But I strongly urge you to at least make an effort to read the Bible as well.

That being said, I think there are some important principles for anyone to follow who is interested in exploring and learning more about "Christianity".

5
The Principles

"Now by the help of these principles, all material things seem to have been composed of the hard and solid particles, above-mentioned, variously associated in the first creation by the counsel of an intelligent agent.

For it became Him who created them to set them in order. And if He did so, it's unphilosophical to seek for any other origin of the world, or to pretend that it might arise out of a chaos by the mere laws of nature; though being once formed, it may continue by those laws for many ages."
- Sir Isaac Newton

The principles I am writing about are not the ones mentioned in the quote on the previous page. The following principles aren't mandatory steps or rules you have to follow. There is no checklist you have to complete. They are just foundational ideas that helped me process and understand what I was reading.

It is my hope that they will make your Bible reading, and investigation into building your own relationship with God, that much more enjoyable. I know from my own personal experience that it can seem like an intimidating book and a daunting task, so having these principles in mind might make it easier to navigate.

But please do not let any one of them become an obstacle to deter you from reading. I do not want anyone to delay reading because they are not able to embrace principle 2, for example. If you find these principles helpful, that is fabulous, but if you do not, that is great too. Let me repeat, there is nothing you have to do or be in order to read the Bible. Please. Just. Start. Reading.

6
PRINCIPLE I
Release who you think you have to be

"I am a Christian person, and I do love the Lord, and I feel no matter who you are, what you believe, how you live your life, it's not my place to judge. I don't have that power. I don't want that power. It's my place to love and to show God's love to other people, even if they don't live a life like I live."
- Carrie Underwood

It really does not matter who you are, or how you identify yourself, or what your current beliefs are, nothing should prevent you from reading the Bible for yourself. If the logic discussed in the previous section has you even the slightest bit curious, you owe it to yourself to find out more. After all, this could impact you for all eternity! In my view, the logical arguments point strongly to believing in what the Bible says because such belief has the highest probability of a positive outcome. Logical investigation of the claims it makes can be done by anyone.

Especially now, with the internet, every barrier to access is being broken down. You don't even have to leave your house! You don't have to spend any money! You don't even have to know how to read! Maybe it is hard to read the small print. There are apps and websites that will read it to you. There are so many churches and organizations that will give out free copies if you are in need. There are several sites with free online Bibles. If some parts are difficult to understand, there are plenty of videos, blogs, and websites that will help explain it to you. You can quickly look up meanings of words or the history of the time period.

The Bible wasn't written only for the "holy people". You don't have to become a wizard to read Harry Potter. You don't have to become a certain kind of person to read the Bible. You don't have to give anything up, you don't have to commit to anything. Just sit down and start reading. No one on this planet is perfect, and we are all sinners, yet we all have the right to read and learn about God and His plan for our lives.

Don't be afraid to start reading because you think you have to clean your life up and quit being "sinful" first. Being "sinless" is actually impossible for any of us, so if you wait until you are perfect and pure to start reading the Bible, it will never happen. Bring your addictions, your greed, your anger, and envy with you while you read!

And here is the secret a lot of people don't realize about the Bible. The "heroes" people talk about? They were all simply regular people like you and me! They were not perfect - just wait until you read about some of the terrible things they did! These parts of the Bible were not written to glorify them or their behavior, they were written to demonstrate how God can act through faithful men and women, even if those faithful men and women are not perfect. They also demonstrate how we can be forgiven for the awful things we have done and how we can repent and learn from our mistakes. Furthermore, their lives serve as examples to the rest of us so that we can learn lessons from both their successes *and* their failures.

Like so many of you, I was afraid that I had done too many bad things and could never make it to heaven, so why even bother, right? I assumed that if I did read the Bible, it would just confirm what I already knew - I was doomed. And sometimes, while I was reading, I would panic for a moment because something hit a little too close to home, but then I would eventually breathe a sigh of relief as I continued reading and learning more. You are not perfect. I am not perfect. No one in the Bible is perfect, except for God. The great news is, you don't have to be perfect to read the Bible! No matter how badly you have sinned, or how horrible you think you are, the Bible is for you.

Notes

7
Principle II
Separate religion from the Bible

"I think there's a distinction between being religious — adhering to the customs created by man, oftentimes appropriating the awe reserved for who I believe is a very real God — and using it to control people, to take money from people, to abuse children, to steal land, to justify hatred. Whatever it is. The evil that's in the heart of every single man has glommed onto the back of religion and come along for the ride."
- Chris Pratt

Take everything you have ever experienced in a house of worship, take every stereotype you have heard about religious people and the religious sects that you are aware of, every ritual, every belief, and toss them out. Start with a fresh, new, open mind. Begin with a blank slate so you do not inadvertently allow a past experience with an inaccurate person or religion to get in the way of your learning from God's word.

We all know people who claim to be Christians but then act in very un-Christian ways. We all have heard horror stories of abuses and scandals in the churches, up to the highest levels. Many of us may have experienced these ourselves. It can be extremely difficult, if not impossible, to understand how someone could claim to follow Jesus but then act in these awful ways. So I completely get that what I am asking is not a simple task for many people.

Reading a book that people have told you will only end by condemning your lifestyle and condemning you to eternal suffering? That honestly does not sound like a fun read at all. But did you know that most of the people claiming to be following the Bible have never actually read the entire book? They copy a few lines from the Bible, out of context, and then use them to judge and condemn everyone but themselves. I was one of those guilty people using quotes out of context to support whatever argument I was making at the time. I know I'm not the only one!

These same things even happened during Jesus' lifetime. The Pharisees and the Sauducees were two prominent Jewish religious sects at that time. Their leaders were very proud, supremely religious men, staunchly following their interpretation of biblical law and determining punishment for those who disobeyed. For example, they contorted God's directive for the sabbath into a means of controlling, judging, and punishing the Jewish masses. They put their own ideas of religion above God's word, including clamoring for the death of Jesus Christ. They were the very definition of the word, "hypocrite".

Sometimes though, the religious person you meet really believes in, and is pursuing, a relationship with God. This does not mean that they suddenly become "perfect". They will still struggle with all of the same things they did before finding God. They might get angry, they might be judgemental, they will make mistakes. But the promise is, if they keep pursuing and turning to God *first,* every time they act that way, they will make progress. So you may run across someone who is trying to follow the Bible, but perhaps you just caught them at the wrong moment. Even the disciples got it wrong sometimes, and acted or spoke in ways contrary to what Jesus wanted them to do. We cannot let other imperfect humans control our behavior and belief.

As for the people who scream about how righteous they are and how much better they are than you, well, I pray they start reading their Bible and learn how their judgment of others will eventually be turned onto their own heads. I also pray that *their* behavior doesn't prevent *you* from following through on investigating the most logical path.

So many people have been successfully prevented from reading the Bible because of what they have seen or heard from people who claim to be followers. But, harsh truth: it is time to grow up and stop using other people's behavior as an excuse for how you live your own life. The

Bible is freely available for anyone to read at any time, so you have the only information you need to find out for yourself. No church, no other person, no religion, can teach you what reading the Bible can.

You have the intelligence to not let the potentially false interpretations of other people cloud your own judgment. Clear your head and go in with very few to no expectations. I would suggest that the only expectation worth having is to "see for yourself" what all of the fuss is about. To learn as much as possible so that you can make up your own mind without the influence of others. There are no preparations you need to make or things you need to fix about yourself first. You can start now.

NOTES

8
Principle III
Make the dedicated effort to read the entire Bible

"These men's writings do not read like the works of gullible, easily deceived or deceiving men. Their insights into human nature are profound. Their personal commitment is sober and carefully stated. Their teachings are coherent and do not look like the invention of unstable men. Their moral and spiritual standard is high. And the lives of these men are totally devoted to the truth and to the honor of God."
- John Piper

Look, I really just want you to begin reading the Bible every day. So whatever it takes for you to get started, please, by all means, follow whatever plan you feel suits you best. Please also use whatever translation you prefer. There are free Bible sites that have several translations so you can read through or research what the best translations are and then choose your favorite. Just make the commitment to read the whole book.

But, in case anyone is curious, here is what I did the first time I tackled the Bible. I am a go-in-order, follow the steps kind of person (which makes me great at unjamming the office copier) so I was determined to start at Genesis and read all the way through in the order it was presented. I didn't realize the books are not always in chronological order the first time I read, so be aware that you may need to look at the timeline of events to put things in order. I was definitely worried I would not understand most of it, or it would be boring. Turns out, I understand much more than I expected, but I still have to look up a lot, and well, parts of it are kind of boring, but most of the stories are actually pretty interesting, and many are downright crazy!

I first had to decide which version to read. I had some idea in my head that I wanted a translation that was a good balance between the most accurate and true to the original language, but also very readable. Some versions are more difficult to read than others. So, because I know absolutely nothing about the various translations and versions of the Bible, I started online. I searched Bible translation review websites and eventually seemed to find that the New American Standard Bible best fit what I had in mind. I think it would be a great idea for everyone else to follow a similar process to find your own preferred translation.

My husband and I each are currently reading out of different versions and it is interesting to compare the language as we study together. There isn't much difference, and the ideas are communicated similarly, although there may be a time when one uses a stronger word that gives a slightly different undertone. We often have interesting discussions when these differences pop up.

Anyway, I started reading and I was going after it every chance I got. I was fired up and dedicated to figuring this out once and for all. I was sick of seeing people use the Bible in online arguments and not knowing for myself what was right or wrong. I wanted to KNOW what the Bible actually said, and there was only one way to do that - read it myself. I was determined to look up anything I didn't understand, and to **read it like it was real** to experience for myself what it would mean for life if it was true. This might sound out there, but really it is no different than what I do when I read any good book. I imagine how it would feel to be a character in the story and I end up laughing or crying along with them. It helps to make stories come alive. So that is also how I read the Bible, imagining what the people must have felt. Pretending to be in their situations and thinking about what I might do in the same circumstances.

    When I came to problematic areas, I wrestled with them. I searched the internet to read several different opinions and listened to various pastors speak about their meaning or importance. This was amazingly helpful, because I learned a few things about the history and cultures that existed during those time periods, and it helped me better understand why people were acting in certain ways.

Being dedicated to it meant I did not stop until I finished the entire Bible, and I read as often as possible. I also put forth the effort to apply it to my life. This was not always easy, as it was so much more obvious to me to find things that other people needed to change or fix. But when I shifted my focus to self-reflection and personal application, and prayed through the lessons and what they meant for me, that is when my real growth started. I made time to read it, I made it a priority in my life. And it changed me.

Many people say you don't have to read the Old Testament first. I personally do not agree with that, as I'll explain below, but I certainly understand why people feel that way. Most often, people start with the New Testament because they find it much easier to read and understand. The language is more modern and it is exciting to read the words of Jesus. This is an historical text, as well as a guide to following God, so it does take some work on the reader's part to understand. The comparisons to things we no longer use, or the concept of different professions or tasks can be difficult to relate to our modern lives. If you can be dedicated to really "getting into it" and trying to make the stories come alive, you will get so much more out of it.

However, none of that means you do not have to read the Old Testament. There are so many examples of faith, and stories with impactful lessons for us to learn from in the Old Testament. It is definitely more difficult to read and likely contains more concerning text, so you will probably take much longer to read through each book. It is worth the effort! In fact, many of the stories you might recognize are found there, such as Daniel in the lion's den, or Samson and Delilah. I know, at least for me, it was exciting each time I reached a story that I vaguely recalled from my time in church.

Taking the time to read and understand the Old Testament is extremely valuable. The Old Testament was all that Jesus and the disciples had ever read, because they were the ones who eventually wrote the New Testament, so they could only use the Old to teach others about God and Jesus. It is what they studied and memorized. I have heard others say that starting with the

New Testament is like starting a movie that is already more than halfway over. A lot of it won't make sense and you might make some erroneous assumptions.

The Bible is by no means an easy read, if you are trying to thoroughly understand it. Sure, you could probably read through it all relatively quickly, but if you do, you will only skim the surface of what it contains. Dedicate yourself to working all the way through every page, delving into areas of confusion, and you will come away with so much more knowledge and wisdom.

Notes

9
Principle IV

Consider the possibility of prayer to help you understand

"What I love about prayer is that in that moment I am 'just' a child of God. Not that famous actor, not the husband of, not the father, but simply a man in contact with his Maker. Prayer, as it were, stops time. God is then number 1 and I only after that. This helps me to see life in a different perspective. To leave my past and future behind and above all to really live in the present."
   – Matthew McConaughey

As I mentioned above, I tried to research parts of the Bible that led me to questions. This greatly helped me to understand what I read and I learned so many things. But the main thing I eventually started doing, and what turned out to help me the most, was praying.

I wasn't really sure how or what to pray at first. In the past, when I got scared or worried about something, I might do a quick prayer saying thank you to God and then asking Him to keep us all safe, happy, and healthy. Later, as I continued my study, my prayers changed to asking God to give me the understanding, knowledge, and wisdom to learn what everything meant. I eventually learned that there is no wrong time to pray and no right way to do it. God just wants us to talk with Him.

I know praying can seem like a strange or intimidating thing to do, especially for those who do not quite believe just yet. Talking to someone you aren't even sure exists absolutely sounds weird! But, once again, there isn't a downside. You can talk to God in your head, or out loud, whatever works for you. When you pray, really try to focus on sharing your heart with God, and feeling and believing that you are talking to God as you pray. If He is real, you might be surprised at what happens. If He is not real, then you will not be out any money, or anything at all, other than a minute of your time. Eventually, you will learn the truth, because you can't stay on the fence forever, but for now I am happy if you just keep open to the idea!

If you aren't sold on the idea of prayer, you could try something like this when you begin your studies, and whenever you come to more difficult parts:

God, if you are real and you really do want me to read this Bible, please let me know this by giving me the knowledge and ability to understand it, so that I can learn what it means. Please come to me and explain it and point me in the right direction, because this part makes no sense to me.

Thank You for Your help and guidance God. Amen.

No risk: either He isn't real and you just thought or said some words, or He is real and He will assist you.

When I first started reading the Bible and listening to sermons, I often found myself praying because my husband, or someone at work or church really needed to learn certain lessons. I was reluctant to fully admit that the lessons applied equally to me. I highly recommend that you begin right away with the plan of applying every lesson to yourself. After you finish a section, pray and ask Him to show you how He wants you to apply it in your own life. Once I started praying about *my* behavior instead of everyone else's, suddenly the world got brighter. My faith was continually replenished and growing, and I was learning so much about God's plans and what our role is in this battle. He continually helps me grow every day.

    I prayed constantly while reading to help me understand and apply the lessons in my own life. By praying and reflecting on what I was reading and what was also happening in my own life, it all started to make so much more sense. The Bible encourages us to pray without ceasing. You may not get the answers to your prayer the first time you pray it. This doesn't mean it didn't work or that God will not answer you. It might mean that it has already started working and the next time you sit down to read, you find the current section easier to understand. It might mean that a few days from now, you will suddenly get insight into something that was bothering you. If you keep at it, you will learn how to acknowledge the results of your prayer. Repeat the above prayer or come up with your own, and feel free to do this as often as you want to while reading. Jesus also gave us the perfect Lord's Prayer to pray and reflect on its meaning, another wonderful way to pray each day. The more often you pray, the better your understanding will have the chance to be, and the more you will learn.

Of course, if you are adamantly opposed to prayer, please do not allow this principle to become a stumbling block to your investigation of the Bible. As I have said before, none of these principles is required when you are first starting to learn. I have included this principle because it so clearly helped me in my personal studies. Perhaps it is just something you keep in your back pocket in case you decide later that prayer is something you are willing to try. You will need to do what is right for you. I do strongly encourage at least trying the prayer above though, just to see what happens!

Notes

10
Principle V
Keep an open mind

"When we come to the Bible and try to listen to its claims, we can easily misjudge those claims if we hear them only from within the framework of our own modern assumptions. Letting the Bible speak for itself, that is, letting it speak in its own terms, includes letting the Bible speak from within its own worldview rather than merely our own."
- Vern Poythress

The Bible was written by many people over a long span of time. It is very cut and dry and most of the time, it does not give much backstory. There are several shocking stories throughout, language that is used that does not make sense to us, commands that are given that sound horrifying. But I encourage you to continue to read and press on. Remember that this book is purported to be describing real life events and, well, real life gets pretty messy at times. It only takes 5 minutes of flipping through online videos or watching the news to see just how messy things can get!

Consider for a moment a history book. History books, along with newspapers, describe the events that happened. The good, the bad, and the ugly. In fact, we complain when these texts do not describe the ugly side of history strongly enough for our liking. We do not condemn a history book or a newspaper for reporting about murder, rape, kidnapping, or slavery. Yet, so many people refuse to even crack open the Bible because they have heard that it contains stories of famous biblical figures doing some pretty awful things. The Bible, just like a good history book or newspaper, does not sugar coat the events that occurred. However, the Bible does something that those other texts do not; it teaches us a way to improve.

If you recall, I wrote earlier about how God uses regular, everyday, imperfect people. So it really shouldn't come as much of a surprise that these people did some scandalous things in their lifetimes. Who among us would love to show our friends and families a movie reel of every one of our most salacious or embarrassing moments? The vileness of society often described or alluded to also shouldn't surprise us. People have been corrupt and evil throughout all time, and we are no different now. For example, for a while, it seemed like every other day the United States FBI was uncovering another child sex-trafficking ring, rescuing hundreds of children. If that wasn't a great enough sign of a depraved society, there are new horrors to be seen every day.

Many of us don't want to read the Bible because we ask, "How could a benevolent God allow all of these horrible things to happen?" But instead of trying to figure out the answer, we just assume the investigation is over at that point. We simply consider that question the end of the discussion and look no further into the issue. This makes no sense. At no stage of my life have I learned something without even bothering to try. I also can't believe I ever just left a giant question like that sitting there with no answer. What *does* the Bible have to say about that issue and others like it?

God judges things as wrong, but by reading the Bible we begin to learn and understand why people behave in these ways and what we need to do to change things. We also learn about the hope and rescue He provides us. I strongly encourage you to write down and then actively seek out answers to all of your burning questions. As you read, try to figure out how each story relates to you and to your questions. If you are open to prayer, ask God to help you find the answers.

Many things that don't make any sense at first will make more sense later when you read about something else. You will begin to make connections between something you remember reading and something you are reading now. If you persevere and read the entire Bible, you will make connections between the Old and New Testament. I found it so beneficial to have read the Old

Testament first, because it helped me understand the mindset of the Jewish people when Jesus arrived. All of the pieces of the puzzle kept falling into place and even now, as I continue to read, it continues to make more and more sense.

The Bible is set up to do several things. It can show us how some people acted in faith and did what God wanted them to, even though they were sinful people otherwise. It can show us the ways in which people have been tested by God and the types of things we must do to prove and build our faith. It can teach us how people have misinterpreted biblical teachings in the past, and how we can understand what those teachings actually mean. It can give us hope that if the people in the Bible were loved by God in spite of the sinful things they did, perhaps He can love us too. It explains how we were all saved by the sacrifice of Jesus Christ. What it does not do is set forth a perfect world full of perfect people. If you go into reading with expectations of perfection and how to attain it, you will be disappointed. The Bible is about real people and how they listened to, or failed to listen to God. It will be messy and complicated, just like real life.

The Bible teaches us how we are all saved, and what we must do to claim our salvation. It teaches us how to step away from the things that are hurting us and to walk on the path God has for us. As you read, write down your concerns and your questions. Look for connections and answers. Try to refrain from making ultimate judgements that stop you from continuing to read.

Notes

11
Principle VI
Take notes

"I meditate on God's life and I read the scriptures. I read something about Him, go through it and spend a lot of time by myself."
- Jim Caviezel

This doesn't seem like a very important step, but it really is crucial. The Bible is a hearty book and takes some dissection and digestion to comprehend much of it. As you delve into the scripture, it can be extremely helpful to keep a journal of the things that bother you, the inspiration you receive, or the questions you have.

It takes a long time to thoroughly read through the entire Bible. For most people if they dedicate daily time to reading, and if they stop and spend the necessary time to explore areas of confusion, it will take about a year to complete the full book. Taking notes as you read and recording your reflections will help you to remember how you felt, and the questions you had, when you first started reading. As you get further into the scripture, you can look back through to see if any of your questions have been answered, and add your new thoughts and knowledge to your notes.

My personal habit of taking notes as I read has been so helpful, especially as my husband and I have been studying together. We have been able to reference my notes from my first reading as we go along, and it helps to kickstart our discussion. Our thinking didn't have to start all over from square one, and we could expand on the ideas in my notes.

The first time I read, it was a free online Bible. I kept a running log in a cloud-based document I titled simply, "Bible Study", and it helped me process what I was learning. As I took more and more notes, the document grew so large that it took longer and longer to open, so I had to keep creating new documents, Bible Study 2, Bible Study 3, etc. There is quite a lot to discover in this text!

For my current read-through, I have a beautiful, physical, note-taking Bible that my husband gave me for Christmas, and I can write directly in it. I wasn't sure at first that I would be comfortable writing notes in the margins, but now that I have let go and given it a try, I absolutely love it! If you are able to get a Bible with space to take notes, I think you would enjoy it once you get used to it. I do have to say, I am glad that I didn't start using this note-taking version until after I had already read it through once, as I am able to be more intentional about what I write. The online documents allowed me to edit mistakes and add as much as I wanted, while obviously the space in the physical copy is limited. I continue to add to my notes in my online documents as well, when I want to write more than space allows. I love having both options available!

So now that you know how I took notes, please know that there is no right or wrong way for you to take notes. Simply grab a pen and notepad, or a tablet with a blank word document, or a Bible with space for notes, or a voice memo recorder, or whatever works best for you. No special format is required, just put your thoughts down so that you can come back to them later and recall them accurately. If you are the type of person who wants to make outlines and columns and headings, go for it! But don't let the product deter you from the process - don't waste the majority of your time on formatting when you should be reading. I found it best to just write. No attempt at organization or sections or anything, just page after page of notes. The only change I might have made, would be to have dated each entry.

Don't focus on having to write something down while you are reading. At some point, something you read will pop out at you. When that happens, take a moment to record that in your notes. You might question something that sounds offensive, so you look up what other people have said about those passages. After you learn a few perspectives, it would be great to add that information to your journal, possibly even with links or quotes from resources you found especially helpful. Or perhaps you might have a word you want to look up, and you add the definition to your notes. There is nothing too big or small to take note of, you never know what will be helpful later on, for you or someone else.

    While reading, I often recognize something similar in the scripture to what is happening in my own life. After some trial and error, I hopefully am able to figure out the lesson the Bible was trying to teach me through those particular passages, and I am able to see how to apply that in my current situation. I write in my notes what the events were, what my role in them was, any repentance I needed to make, any prayers I prayed, any lessons I learned. The more I read, the more I was able to make sense of my previous notes. Things I would not have remembered were written down for me to synthesize with the new information I was reading. Studying the Bible became exponentially easier and everything was more comprehensible. Even if I didn't reference my notes and re-read them often, the act of writing down my thoughts helped me to reflect on them and recall them as I read further.

Do not censor your notes. Think of them more as a brainstorming exercise than a final thesis. Do not worry about what you write being correct or incorrect. Your notes really should simply be your raw, real, nitty-gritty questions, concerns, ideas, thoughts, and impressions as you read through this book. As you continue to read, your notes will grow and change, as they also guide you. Find what works best for you.

Notes

12
PRINCIPLE VII
Don't set unrealistic goals and expectations

"My heart wants to read the Bible, wants to obey God. When you have Jesus in your life, when you have God in your life, like the thing in this world is not important to your heart. The more important is God in your heart. That's how God changed my life."
- Manny Pacquiao

When you make the decision to start reading the Bible, and you begin looking for information on how to read it, you will probably come across several sites claiming to have "The Best Bible Study Plan!" They will set up page a day plans, or plans centered around a theme, with daily reading goals. They will reward you with reading streaks if you read so many days in a row, and they will chastise you when you blow your streak. Many allow you to read with other people, such as your church study group, tracking one another's progress and leaving notes for the group on inspiring passages. If this is your thing, and you know this type of motivation will work for you, then please go ahead! I know that you will use the motivational tools in a positive way to guide your reading, and will not let something like missing a day deter you.

Unfortunately though, in my experience, apps and plans like this only seem great at first. I start off excited and eager and ready to read all of the passages assigned for the first week on the first day. I keep up a great pace for a while and get my weekly streak bonus and I'm so proud of what a great job I'm doing. Then I miss a day because the kids and the husband have one too many activities pulling me in one too many directions and I fall asleep before I even have a chance to read. No worries, I start my streak over and I am at it again, but then more and more days come where I can't meet the goal. I fall further and further behind, and I haven't even had time to figure out what that reading from last Thursday meant! Before long, I feel so far behind that even looking at the icon for the app makes me feel guilty and annoyed, so I just stop completely. I feel defeated that I couldn't keep up with the program and assume there must be something wrong with me.

 I found instead, it worked best for my personal circumstances to just make a goal to read something from the Bible each day. I did not follow any plan or program. I merely made sure I read at least one or two sentences every day. Although there were days when even that felt like too much effort, when I forced myself to start to read, I often found that I wanted to continue reading.

 I do not want to dissuade anyone from using one of those reading programs. Those apps can be a wonderful and motivating tool for so many people. If they help even one person, that is all that matters. I just write about my own experiences to caution anyone who might be like me, to be careful.

In my opinion, trying to stick to anyone else's pace for daily reading is not the most effective way to read the Bible. Some people need more time to grapple with certain stories or concepts than others, and will need to re-read and research before moving on. You could always use the programs to give you a guide, but ignore the arbitrary goals for how much to read each day.

The Bible is not meant to be a simple, quick read. It is meant to be a complex, living work that we apply to our lives as we read it. This may mean that certain passages take you longer to unpack. Some might resonate with you more than others and lead you to re-read them several times. Some might require a lot of research and wrestling with the information. So there is no way to predict how long it will take to read any set number of pages. There were some days where I might have only read one sentence. The best advice is to strive for a mindset of a daily, intentional, go where the reading leads type of plan. If that means you are re-reading that same one paragraph from yesterday and then looking up and learning more about it today, then that may be all you do. There may be no new passage for the day because you are still working through the passage from the day before. Whatever pace you need to follow is the right pace.

Your only goal should be to read the Bible every day. Please don't fall into the trap of setting goals for the number of pages you will read, or the weekly total number of minutes. This will only set you up for failure and disappointment, which could eventually discourage you from finishing. Read what you can each day and give yourself credit for the time you spend working through each page.

Notes

13

PRINCIPLE VIII
Don't stop

"There was a battle in my brain—in my soul—and I wasn't sure who I was going to let win. This wasn't the drugs talking to me; this was something different. It was almost like—well, it sounds weird—but it was almost like God and the devil were fighting over my soul. Like it was a spiritual fight for my life, but it was up to me to make the final choice."
- Brian Welch

The Bible is a very hearty, very unique book. As I mentioned before, it takes most people a long time to read the entire book the first time, especially if they are dedicated to understanding it. Considering it might take a year to read, a lot can happen in our lives during that time frame. It is critical to be aware of this fact, so that you can be prepared and have a plan in place to overcome the obstacles that will prevent you from reading. Make the decision that no matter what happens, you will continue to pick up reading until you have completed the entire book.

You might start off with the best intentions to read an hour a day, every day. And you do for a while. But over the course of a year, there are going to be days when everything is going wrong. You will be in a rotten mood and the last thing you will want to do is read. You might become ill or injured and unable to read for a time. You might just become stuck on a tedious, difficult passage and lose your steam.

Whatever the case, there is only one way to get over those obstacles to reading, and it may surprise you. If you have lost your desire or are having trouble getting motivated to read the Bible, you have to…..read the Bible! The desire to read the Bible comes from reading the Bible. The more you read it, the more you will want to continue reading. The hardest step on those rough days is simply getting started.

When you are having a horrible day and you don't want to read, start by taking a moment for a time-out. Thirty seconds to walk into a quiet space and breathe. Focus on calming and if you are open to prayer, ask God to give you peace, and to quiet your mind so that you may read and focus on His word for a few minutes. Then take another 60 seconds or so and get yourself to read just one or two sentences. If you feel like reading more, go for it. When you finish, process what you just read for another moment. It is possible that it might apply or have some bearing on what you are facing today. If so, consider how you can use this lesson. If it doesn't, simply reflect on what it did say. We do not always receive ground-breaking insight from every verse we read. Just appreciate that you were able to find a minute or two to read and then start each day fresh.

If you get off track, don't sweat it, just get back on track right away. Don't wait until later. The moment you realize you haven't read the Bible recently, find some way to go read a quick passage. Eventually, you will build up to a solid daily reading time again.

There are going to be stories that are so interesting that you finish the whole section in one sitting, and other parts that seem to go on forever about nothing important. Your life will also have its natural ebbs and flows over the months as you are reading. The frequency and volume of your study will vary greatly throughout that time. The only plan is to remain committed to finishing the entire book. Don't ever stop completely!

My favorite times to read are first thing in the morning, at lunch, and before bed. My life gets exponentially better each time I read and study. But, I still miss days even though I know I shouldn't. I want to read more often than I do, but I am also great at making excuses. I am a busy wife and mom of busy kids and I work full-time, so it isn't difficult to find ways to avoid reading. All of the advice in this book is advice I give myself, because it was born out of my experiences and notes and inspiration as I was reading the Bible for the first time. I have learned so many amazing things through trial and error, so it is my hope that these principles will encourage you to delve more deeply into your biblical study. When you do that, it makes it far more likely that you will finish, and you will find that while life may get a little topsy-turvy, you remain invested in your study and you don't allow roadblocks to prevent you from reaching your goal.

When you lose steam, just keep your focus on the end goal. This is a long-term project, so you will have setbacks as well as powerful moments. As long as you persevere and don't ever completely stop reading, you *will* be able to reach your goal of reading the entire book.

Notes

14
Principle IX
Consider looking for support

"You need to have the guidance of someone else. You can not train yourself. I feel the same way about Christianity and what the Church is : The Church is the gym of the soul."
- Sylvester Stallone

"Let us seek friends that will stir up our prayers, our Bible reading, our use of time, and our salvation."
- J. C. Ryle

When I first started reading the Bible, I was pretty much on my own as far as the actual reading. At the time, no one in my family or friend group was reading with me. I preferred it that way because I wanted to wrestle with the text on my own first. I wanted to at least have a basic understanding and to have read through the entire book at least once before I felt comfortable discussing much with others. I was always the type of person who doesn't like to be wrong. I initially wanted to know as much as I could so I could minimize the chances of embarrassing myself. That concern actually supplied me with the willpower to read whenever I could, because I was reading to satisfy my own need to know the truth of what the Bible actually said.

This plan of individual study generally worked out pretty well for me, because I was strongly motivated to read and figure things out. I didn't need motivation from other people, or a goal to complete before meeting my study group in order to keep me reading and inspired. I also wasn't entirely on my own, in addition to God's divine inspiration, I found some excellent online sermons and teachings that provided insight into the scripture I was reading. I sought out several sources and speakers and compared what they said to what I was reading.

This support made my comprehension possible. Without listening to the voices of others on these topics, I would have had a much more difficult time making sense of what I read. I learned to look at each of the events described from the perspectives of everyone involved, not just the main person. I learned details about the underlying events of the time periods, and explanations of the customs and traditions of each culture.

I did also begin attending a church regularly during that time. My family started watching online at first, and eventually we went in person once quarantines were over and places were allowed to reopen. It was amazing to me how often the sermon for the day would match up with what I had just been reading. So many times I'd tell my husband, "I was just reading that last night!" You may find this happening as well while you are reading, if you are also seeking out other resources to support your study. I found it sort of acted like a confirmation and reinforcement of what I was learning, and gave me greater insight into each passage whenever it happened.

As I really started getting into the scripture, I think that the weekly sermons I was being given through church were highly beneficial. Learning from people who were much more knowledgeable than me, and hearing interpretations that made the stories come to life in an even more colorful way really had a huge impact on my knowledge. There were often viewpoints I had never considered that suddenly and completely changed the way I understood a story. If you can track down a good Bible study group or church in your area, you may find it to be a critical resource to understanding some of the more hidden and elusive facets of the biblical stories.

Once again, this all comes down to a matter of personal preference. I don't want to deter anyone from starting to read because they have to find a good study group first. Start reading, and at the same time, start looking for resources that might be most helpful to you. I have not put any specific recommendations for any resources in this book because I do not want it to seem like I am suggesting that you attach your biblical studies and research to one particular line of thinking or person. Too often people put their faith in the hands of a certain pastor, or people at church, and they start to rely on them instead of reading God's Word for themselves. Let me make it clear that in my opinion, solely attending church is not enough to know what God wants for us. We have to read His Word. The focus should be on learning what the Bible says, and any other resources you use should be for support and understanding only. You should never put your own study on the back burner and switch all of your investigation and focus onto the teachings of someone else. People are fallible and can have varying motives and agendas. If you rely too heavily on one particular person, group, or resource, you may lose sight of what the text actually says, and become bogged down in the dogma of whatever or whomever you have been relying on instead of the Bible itself.

    That being said, I do think that at some point in your studies, it is important to connect yourself with others who are studying the Bible. There is something special that occurs when people get together and talk about what they learned while reading a particular passage, or when someone explains how God has done things in their life. We can read and get an understanding of what each of the stories mean, but when we share our thoughts with others, this is when the Bible truly comes to life.

Joining a Bible study group also does not mean that you are committing to any particular religion or belief system. Many churches would love to have someone new join their group (don't bother with the ones who don't, just look for one that does). There are also often groups connected with schools or workplaces so people who do not feel comfortable walking into a church might feel more at ease sitting in a classroom or cafe. If you cannot find a study group that welcomes everyone or suits your needs, why not start one yourself? Most public libraries will allow residents to use their community room for free for non-commercial use. This is what my husband and I did when we started our study group. We wanted everyone to feel as though they could come and read what the Bible says without worrying about sitting through a church service or prayers and sermons. We were hoping for believers, and non-believers, and maybe-believers to come together and learn. Hopefully you can find something like that near you, but creating your own is always a fabulous option!

Side note: How do you know if a resource or study group/church is "good" and reliable? Well, praying for guidance is always a great choice! But in general, it is quite simple: compare what is being taught with what the Bible says. If it looks to be a match, then all is probably well. If not, continue to investigate to see if it is a matter open to interpretation or a mistake. If you find that there is consistent discord between the Bible and any source, then that source would not be worthwhile to look at as a representation of biblical application or interpretation. This is why it is so crucial for you to read the Bible for yourself. There are so many false teachers who exist to mislead us about the Word of God, whether intentionally or not. Knowing when something doesn't mesh with the Bible becomes very important to protecting the integrity of what you are learning.

Find a means of support that is most beneficial to supporting your studies. Look for resources and learning communities that can supplement what you are reading.

They can all help to strengthen your commitment, keep you motivated, and guide you to understanding.

Notes

15
I FINISHED! WHAT NEXT?

"The first thing I do when I start my day is, I get down on my hands and knees and give thanks to God. Whenever I go outside of my house, the first thing I do is stop at the church."
- Mark Wahlberg

Congratulations! By reading the entire Bible, you have accomplished something many people never will. I hope that the principles in this book proved helpful to you as you read. I pray that you are now convinced of its truth and are eager to continue your journey. There are several steps you can take to help you grow in your faith from this point, so I will not spend too much time on each of them. That could be an entire book in itself, and probably is in one form or another!

You have already taken a huge step by reading the Bible.

Now read it again!

I know it might seem like I'm kidding, but I'm not! Even though we have read it all the way through, we should continually read from it every single day, so that we can remember it well enough to carry it with us in our day to day lives. In fact, I believe this to be one of the most common reasons that people who claim to be "Christian" end up misrepresenting what the Bible says. I strongly suspect that most of them are not reading their Bible daily. They end up watching programs that use biblical verses out of context to support a particular political view or mindset instead of looking to the book itself. They listen to the world more than the Word.

When we do not read daily, we leave room for our minds to forget exactly what the Bible says. This in turn creates the opportunity for us to be led astray. We end up seeking out people and resources that align with what we think sounds best, not realizing that it doesn't align with the Bible. In our minds we believe that we are doing the right thing, but since we haven't read, or it has been a while, we don't realize that we are sometimes doing the exact opposite of what the Bible says for us to do. We end up with a misguided and mistaken view of what God wants, and many times that leads to some pretty poor behavior, and/or judgment of others.

Reading daily also gives us the armor we need to face all of the small and big issues that come up in our lives each day. If you get into the habit, you may find that reading, for just a few moments even, will often turn a dark mood around instantly. Almost every time I read, I end up with a lesson, a solution, some inspiration, or advice that lines up perfectly with whatever was on my mind at that time. You will learn or notice something new each time you read it. You will be surprised at some of the things you thought you remembered, but now you notice something different. It will not feel like reading the same book twice!

The other most important thing is prayer. By now, if you have made it this far, you may be either furiously typing up a scathing review of this book, or you are thinking about earnestly pursuing a relationship with God. I am expecting in faith that most of you will be the latter, but either way, prayer is your friend. Praying every day, starting and ending your day by talking to God, well, it makes sense that it could only help you. As I said above, there are no rules to praying. You can see how Jesus prayed in the Bible. You can come up with your own prayers, or just talk to Him. Thank Him, ask Him, seek Him.

If you have decided you are ready to make the choice to believe in God, and the sacrifice, death, resurrection and saving of your soul by Jesus Christ, there is something called the sinner's prayer. Many churches invite people to pray some version of this prayer at the end of the service if they have made the decision to turn their life over to God. I created a mash-up of what I liked best about the several versions I have seen/heard:

Lord, my God,

I admit that I am a sinner and that I have sinned against You and my neighbors. I have not loved You with my whole heart and I have not treated my neighbors as I would treat myself. I am truly sorry and I humbly repent all of my sins. I ask that You in Your infinite grace and mercy, please forgive me. I believe that You in Your unending love sent Your only Son to come to rescue me, and I believe that Jesus Christ went to the cross to die for my sins. I believe that His death and resurrection saved me from death and brought me into eternal life with You. Please come into my life and into my heart and change me. Fill me with Your Holy Spirit. Teach me to trust and follow You. You chose to die for me; from this day forward, I choose to live for You.

Amen.

In addition to reading the Bible and praying daily, there are so many great options to turn to for guidance in deepening and broadening your faith. Now that you have read the Bible, you will find it easier to look for a church or worship group that teaches directly from it, and you will know if they are saying something that God didn't say. I was attending church as I was reading and the sermons helped bring things to life, and volunteering gave me a place to focus some of my energy and zeal for God for a while as I learned and studied. Finding a strong Bible-based church you can attend is a solid step. Hearing the testimony of other people and listening to someone teach about the nuances and lessons behind the biblical stories is a powerful thing. The fellowship of other people also helps when you encounter dark times and you need support.

    There are also so many wonderful pastors who post their sermons or write articles online. When I first started reading, I was doing some research on Uzziah and I came across some audio-only Bible lessons from the seventies. I found them absolutely fascinating. I started listening to them while I was getting ready for work in the mornings and on my lunch breaks, and I learned so much. There are also lots of books and websites throughout the world on every religious topic. Just be careful to compare whatever you are hearing or reading against what you have read in the Bible, to ensure that you don't accidentally get led astray. Take for example this huge red flag that I actually saw in a best-selling religious marriage book. It told people that they did not have to study the Bible, just so long as they applied the select parts of scripture the author quoted. Here's a hint: Anyone who tells you that you do not have to study the Bible is not your spiritual friend.

The other thing that really helped jumpstart my faith journey was making myself do a 30-day challenge to listen to only the praise and worship radio stations in my car. No matter where I went, no matter who was in the car with me (even my teenagers!), I kept it on those stations for thirty days. At first I did not like it. I love to sing along and I had never heard most of these songs before. Eventually I would hear some that I recognized from church. Then I started to learn a few of the more catchy ones. Now, it is the only kind of music I ever want to listen to. I play it while I clean, while I'm driving, every chance I get. It is very difficult to have a negative outlook when you are singing praise music! And even my teenagers sing along sometimes now too!

Once you have read the entire Bible, you will understand that God never promises His followers an easy life. In fact, we learn that as soon as we make the decision to follow God, we usually begin being attacked even more vigorously by the forces that want to keep us away from His word. The people in the Bible are examples because they learned to praise God no matter what hardships or dangers they were facing. They also learned to look to God first and foremost for help in every situation. Trouble is going to continue to come your way, but the Bible lessons will help you through it. The people in the Bible learned to praise Him in the good times too - we must all remember where we came from! This is why daily practices of faith like reading the Bible, praying, and learning from others help us to remain focused on God and His plans for our lives.

You should also understand that God calls upon His followers to listen to Him and obey His commands. When you start talking to God and learning from Him, He is going to ask you to do things. Our job on this earth, once we know about the gospel, is to tell as many other people as possible. We are supposed to help other people realize what we have realized. He will also test your faithfulness and your willingness to listen and obey. This is one reason there are so many examples of ordinary people stepping out in faith to do whatever crazy thing God has asked them to do. Build a huge ship in the middle of the desert so everyone can think I am crazy? Sure God, no problem! While He probably doesn't need you to build a boat, He may want you to do something equally as outlandish given your circumstances. Are you ready?

As I said, one of the most important things God wants all of his followers to do, is to tell others about Him. Now that you know the scriptures and gospels and are growing in your faith, that is your job too! Be willing to tell others about the impact reading the Bible and developing a relationship with God has made in your life. If you love the people around you, you must want them to also have the best chance to achieve the only possible positive outcome. The only way they can do that is by learning about and developing their own relationship with God. Think about how you might feel if someone you love could have been spared the fate of the outcome of eternal torment, but you never bothered to help them find their way. If you do nothing else, encourage others to study the Bible as you have done.

Ultimately, it is between you and God how you decide to build your relationship. By praying and reading and learning, and listening to what God wants for your life, you will assure yourself the _best_ possible outcome! Thank you for reading, I pray that you found something useful in these pages to support you in your pursuit of God.

The End

"If religious books are not widely circulated among the masses in this country, I do not know what is going to become of us as a nation. If truth be not diffused, then error will be. If God and His Word are not known and received, the devil and his works will gain the ascendancy. If the evangelical volume does not reach every hamlet, the pages of a corrupt and licentious literature will. If the power of the gospel is not felt throughout the length and breadth of this land, anarchy and misrule, degradation and misery, corruption and darkness will reign without mitigation or end."
 - Daniel Webster

Most Holy God,

I pray for every person reading these words that You will call out to them and that they will hear and respond to Your call. I pray that they will read the Bible You have given us and that they will learn and understand Your Word. I pray that they will give their lives over to You. I pray for healing and blessings in their lives as they grow in their walk with You. Thank You for the many blessings You have given me and the miracles You continually work in my life. Every few minutes something reminds me of Your goodness and I am overcome with amazement at how wonderful You are. Please hold onto all of us and watch over us and guide us as we do Your work here on this earth. Thank you Father, in Jesus' name. Amen

Notes

Made in the USA
Monee, IL
24 June 2023